30 DAY DIGITAL AGENCY

Marketing
Networking
Operations
Productivity
Sales
More...

A step-by-step tutorial on what you need to start & run a **successful** digital agency in one month

NICK CALABRO

Preface

Hello all, *30 Day Digital Agency* was written to help you start and grow your digital agency. There has never been a better time to start a digital agency since there are more and more businesses each and every day that can benefit from these services.

This is the business to start if you want to be an entrepreneur because there are no overhead costs and you can get started right now. Starting the agency, getting your first clients, and scaling your agency requires a science that is laid out in here based on how I started and grew Calaboration.

To become a truly efficient entrepreneur, digital agencies are the greatest first step because it allows you to talk to business people, get a feel for the different types of industries, and helps you grow your entrepreneurial mindset.

I hope you enjoy the book and am looking forward to hearing stories of the agencies you build from it.

About The Author

Nick Calabro is the CEO of Calaboration — a digital marketing and media agency located in New Jersey. He graduated from John Jay College with a degree in Computer Science and Public Administration.

Calaboration works with clients from all walks of life including real estate professionals and politicians. By working alone while building the company, Nick has had massive amounts of time to reflect and determine what is truly important in life and what it takes for someone to succeed.

After Nick left his day jobs to become an entrepreneur, he focused heavily on how he can maximize his productivity. He writes about these systems and processes on his blog, EntrepreneurialEfficiency.com.

Introduction

30 Day Digital Agency takes you through the exact steps you can take right now to officially become a digital agency CEO in one month. This book is a compilation of notes, journal entries, and recollections from when I started Calaboration and how we grew it to where it is today.

Starting your own agency could be the most fulfilling thing you ever do and will always remain your business — it helps you build a foundation that you can use to refine your skills and will always be available in case anyone needs a website or digital marketing services no matter what you're doing with your life at the time. Even when opening new businesses or starting new ventures, you can always run some online advertisements for a client here and there.

Whether you're trying to build a large-scale agency or a small-time freelancing career, *30 Day Digital Agency* will get you started in no time.

Why Start a Digital Agency?

Some say there are too many digital agencies. Firstly, this is too heavy of a statement because your digital agency can be such a wide array of things offering a spectrum of different services. There will always be a need for agencies to handle the digital side of things that other businesses cannot handle.

Saying there are too many digital agencies is like saying there are too many real estate agents. Yes, there are many — and yes, there will be a small few that are top performers, but everyone else in between can happily get by and make a living off of it.

Running your very own digital agency is not freelancing. Freelancing is inefficient and as unfulfilling as working a 9-5 job. When you freelance, you trade your time for money which is never a good deal for you — when you run an agency, you negotiate contracts that provide a profit for you while you outsource the work you'd normally be freelancing yourself. In short, an agency allows you to hire freelancers — and eventually employees — to enable you to make more money by selling and managing.

Once your agency is up and running, you may have to eat a few months or even a couple years until you're sustainable enough to hire out work. This will be a trying time for you and your company to determine if you're truly fit to run a business in the first place. Once you make it past this threshold, it's glorious, fun, and profitable — you become the boss of your life.

When you finally build enough of a portfolio and establish systems that allow your company to run without you micromanaging it, you're free to travel and run your company from wherever you desire — these are the benefits of running a digital agency. If you're selling digital services like websites, advertising, or mobile applications, no one will be expecting you to show up at the office on a daily basis and you can manage your team, if you've set in place the proper communication channels, from wherever while you reap benefits.

Starting a digital agency has never been easier and will always give you fast returns. There is no overhead when you're selling a website to your local pizzeria. Merely walk in, propose the deal, and profit. The potential to scale and build your company is entirely up to how much work you put into getting clients who are willing to pay for your services.

Week One: Starting Up

First Steps Before Starting Your Agency

Starting my agency, Calaboration, came pretty naturally to me. Some things were dreadful and others were so simple — I realize everyone struggles in different areas and sometimes they're unsure where to actually begin. Here are the initial steps we took to get my digital agency started.

The first thing you should be doing when starting your digital agency is determining your value proposition. Why is someone going to give you money for this and how is it helping their business's bottom line? Research the niche, the industry, and the current agencies doing what you're trying to do for inspiration.

Before you dive into selling any websites to any clients, determine where you may be most effective. If you went to school for finance, perhaps you should be targeting bankers and financial advisors who may need your services. If you come from a family of real estate agents, perhaps you can gain some industry knowledge in the market and target those clients.

Further, you will need to determine which services you are actually providing. More importantly, you must understand the benefits your client will see by these services.

Planning

We're not going to go into creating business model canvases just yet — this will be an effective exercise but is unnecessary before you've landed your first client. The most you should be doing during your planning phase is merely outlining the services and verticals you want to focus on.

This will consist of some market research and soul-searching on your end. Do some studying and find the markets, industries, or services being offered in your area and how they're doing their marketing — if they're investing in any marketing at all. This will help guide you and expose you to what your prospects want and expect before you even start reaching out to prospects and start selling.

Choose Your Vertical

When you're starting out, it is wise to choose a specific niche or vertical. Although it seems counterintuitive, you will have more results if you target *only* real estate professionals or *only* chiropractors instead of advertising that you can do any marketing strategy for any small to medium-sized business. Everyone needs digital marketing and web design but deciding on a niche and channeling your skills appropriately will be much more effective.

Even though you technically can build a website for any business, niche down anyway and learn to speak the language of a vertical so well that you are the obvious choice if they were looking at multiple agencies. You will find that you will receive more referrals this way since you will be the go-to professional in this given field. Meanwhile, the person that can do any website for anyone will be seen as the less-specialized budget option.

Real estate is an easy vertical since it's so broad and involves many different sub-categories. Real estate includes anyone from general contractors, real estate agents, real estate investors, appraisers, mortgage lenders, and more. You can get by understanding real estate well enough that you can speak the languages, but that might be spreading it too thin as well.

Fields like dentistry, chiropractors, nail salons, and physical therapy are great verticals to focus on for a number of reasons.

1. They're abundant. Nearly every town will have a local dentist or salon.
2. They're likely profitable and sustainable enough to hire out some extra marketing work to be done as well.
3. They're local. This is an edge for you since they'll feel comfortable doing small-scale work with someone who is small-scale enough to be serving businesses in that area. If you're in a large city, you will have to find tinier neighborhoods to achieve this similar phenomenon.
4. They're businesspeople too. This means you will likely find them at local networking events, you can build a rapport, gather referrals, and build trust with them. Further, they will appreciate someone who is starting up a business since it was very likely them only a little while ago when they began their business. This goes back to debunking the myth that high-end professionals hate cold callers. In fact, they love getting cold called (well) because they appreciate the hunger the person on the other end of the phone is displaying.

Think about a conversation you may have with someone who knows prospects for you.

Friend: "Hey, what's your company do?"
You: "We make websites."
Friend: "Oh, cool. I'll let you know if I hear someone needs a website."

vs.

Friend: "Hey, what's your company do?"
You: "We make websites for real estate agents."
Friend: "Oh, I know some real estate agents. I'm sure they'd love to speak with you."

One scenario got you zero leads while the other got you a potential few. When you pick a vertical, you mark your territory and let people know what you're really all about. This friend you were talking to was overwhelmed by the millions of possible solutions you can provide with, simply, "websites". But, when you demonstrated you're focused on a certain niche, they immediately thought of their contacts that could benefit from exactly that.

You may be thinking you're missing out on work by niching down like this. Keep in mind that you do not have to *exclusively* service one specific vertical, but you're only *advertising* for the niche. If you're targeting dentists and a local dive bar asks for a website, don't turn them down. Merely explain that you specialize in real estate but you have the knowledge and tools to service them just as well. They'll be happy that you're willing to go outside your niche for them and they'll feel even more valued as a client as a result of this.

When I was starting my agency, I carried two separate business cards. One that explained we do a wide range of services for one niche, and one that said we do a very specific service for anyone and everyone. Depending who I was speaking to and if they fit within the niche, they'd get that card, everyone else got the other card. This allowed us to grow in different directions and test which service and solutions were working best and which ones there was a larger market for.

Small business is too broad of a niche. I find people sometimes saying how they specialize in digital marketing for small businesses. Okay — you could have a small law firm and a small real estate development company; the marketing services are going to be very different for those. As the agency owner, it's your job to niche down and choose a few areas that you can shine in best.

Learn Their Industry

Once you've settled on a vertical, do all you can to become an expert in that field without actually working in the field. Some of the better real estate marketing agencies are run by people who are real estate investors or who were real estate agents. This allows them to very thoroughly understand the market and perform at maximal levels.

Remember that by investing all this time in the niche without performing in that niche to make money is the key ingredient to making more money. Imagine you're selling websites and marketing to dentists. Sure, you can become a dentist yourself, but you'll eventually need a website and marketing as well. During the gold rush, the people who were selling the clothing and the shovels were the ones that were making all the money because they were selling products and commodities that everyone needed. If you signed twenty local dentists a $5000 website you've just earned more money than most people never even see as their salary.

The investment you make into learning the industry and coming at it from the side-door is worth much more than entering through the front door where everyone else is trying to gain access to. This is exactly what it means to capitalize on the opportunity. There are so many businesses that need to build an online presence, run digital advertising, start email marketing, and even create custom digital solutions. The difference between their business and yours is that you have a commodity that can turn a profit immediately while they're struggling to make sales and close deals.

The real estate industry is the best example of this. You have thousands of people in every city trying to make it big by flipping homes and building a portfolio of investment properties. You can grind for a few years and follow their footsteps in hopes that you may find success in real estate as well — or you can find where all these real estate professionals are hanging out and sell each and every one of them a website and marketing strategy. Further, you've already prequalified these leads because if they're an active investor or agent at all they already have deals in their pipeline that can directly fund your services.

Learn Their Problems

Now that you've settled on which industry you're going to target your services to and did the diligent research, you have to now put yourself in their shoes and understand their pain points and problems. Where are they struggling most in their business that you can have the biggest impact on once they sign on with you?

Imagine a real estate agent. The *only* thing they care about are leads. They want a steady flow of qualified leads coming into their pipeline because it's the one thing that enables them to actually do their job which is following up with them and attempting to sell or list their homes. If you can propose that you will create an online system to do exactly that for them, you'll be golden and they'll sign you right away.

A dentist office might have a very similar pain point. They may want more cleanings scheduled so they can eventually get those clients into larger operations where they can make real money. Your job at that point will be to get more people signing up for cleanings through online advertising. Keep in mind, anyone can get leads — websites and services sell lists of leads at any given time. The value that you're providing these prospects is that they're more qualified leads and that it's more of an untapped market right now since very few dentist offices in the area are utilizing digital marketing.

Further problems prospects might be facing may revolve around digital solutions. If a client is telling you how hard it is to stay on top of past clients through email marketing, that's a solution you can provide by building out an email marketing sequence. Even if they come to you with a specialized problem that requires some custom email system, understand their frustration, assess the core issue, and hire out a developer to create the program if you have to. The bottom line is that you are in front of this client and you have the power, ability, and will to solve their issues using anything digital.

Choose Your Services

Now that you understand your vertical and their problems, you have to consider what you're going to be actually selling them. This can be one of many things or many of one thing. You can sell full-service marketing that involves content, creative, advertising, video, web design, and more — or you can keep it basic and only offer SEO services to your clients. Whichever you choose you have to ensure you know the effects of these systems so you can properly sell them on the results.

Selling one-off websites is going to be the easiest thing to start with. You can learn to spin up a brand new website in the matter of a single weekend and easily promise clients a website in under four weeks once they sign the agreement. Selling websites is great because no one wants to deal with it, you can add and remove feature so you can both agree on a fair price that works for either of you, and just about everyone needs a website — further, just about everyone who already has a website has a poor website that either isn't mobile-friendly, has SEO issues, or is just terribly outdated. Essentially, you can safely tell anyone, without even looking at their website, that you can improve their website.

Websites are also a great gateway into a client's business. Once you build out someone's website and they're happy with it, you can easily upsell them into some marketing services. Now that you have a website up, you have to drive traffic to it. Further, you'll have to continuously work on the SEO so the site doesn't get lost in search engines and is always relevant while people are searching. Never be discouraged by *only* building a client's website — instead, you are given the opportunity to demonstrate your skills and it is up to you to sell them on the bigger and better stuff after you 'wow' them this first time around.

If you want to take a more specialized approach, you can always sell one-off creatives as well. If clients know what they want and they need a video, infographic, or logo, these are things that can easily be done in only a few days by the right agency. Real estate agents will always need photos and videos of their listings. Similarly, your local pizzeria may need some print-media for their menus or signs. Someone has to design those things to be printed and it will nearly certainly not be the business owner.

Selling very specific deliverables like blog posts and videos are a great way to hone in on your craft and master that one niche. You may find it harder to find work at first since the amount of services you're providing is so specific, but that also leaves you open to charging more since you are the best at doing that one little thing. Conversely, full-service agencies have the power to deliver whatever the client asks for since they're going out of their way to handle the digital efforts by any means necessary. However, the video quality of a full-service agency might always be even slightly less impressive than that of a video production shop.

What results are you providing them?

Businesses only care about their bottom line. No one is going to want to hear about how you target an audience and build converting websites — that's too technical for them — they only want to hear about how you will make them more money and in turn give you more money.

Quality leads is something every business wants and needs — real estate agents, especially, need leads coming through because it's the one and the only thing that will enable them to do their job. Forget about doing their job more effectively, leads coming through the door will keep them moving whether they convert or not. Further, quality leads will enable them to do more with these leads and thus allow them to be busy more often with these leads and then it's up to them to convert them.

Qualified leads is a step further from **quality leads**. You can be an interested homebuyer and tour a few houses with a real estate agent but they'll only ever buy that million dollar listing if they're qualified in the first place.

This is where you can up the ante on your services and include that you only target qualified leads and that they're vetted before they even hit the client's inbox.

Foot traffic is something all restaurants and bars need. Again, this is the only thing that increases their bottom line — likes and shares on social media will get them well-known, but that is not money in the bank. likes and shares might be valuable if your client is a talk show or podcast host since any view or download will mean more ad revenue for them.

Getting people in the door of a physical location is paramount for any client that has a physical store. The way to do this is to offer promotions, discounts, and build an incentive for someone to come through the door at all.

Shares and views are useful only for the right type of client. someone who has an ego and wants to be famous online can easily drop thousands of dollars on advertising and not even make any money off it. this is fine for you since you're building their platform and getting paid in the process and as long as their happy with the results, that's all you need to care about

We've had clients that request ego-stroking marketing instead of tactical and strategic marketing. Getting on the first page of a google search for a keyword that barely any of your clients are searching isn't beneficial for anyone. Sometimes they'll think they need that keyword so they can feel good about themselves. You're the expert marketer here, though.

Learn the Benefits of Your Services

Before you learn the mechanics of web design or video production, you have to learn the impact it will have on the type of business vertical you decided on earlier. You are not selling websites and marketing. You are selling a lead generating machine and branding. You are selling the result of what you are providing — no one cares about the code you're using on the website or the SEO tactics you're implementing; they care about the results they'll see on their bottom line once you begin the marketing or whichever services you are providing.

This is beneficial for a number of reasons. If you sold someone on the basis of them getting however many more leads per month, they will be completely disconnected from your process. You'll notice that your first few clients are extremely micromanaging and difficult to work with — this merely comes with the territory of low-ticket clients being the most involved in the process because they want to ensure they're getting the biggest bang for their buck. However, if you keep them out of your process as much as possible and as early as possible you will allow yourself to experiment on your terms and deliver the results however you see fit.

You can imagine issues if you are selling a local physical therapist Facebook advertising and they go for a week without much return. They may decide to take some matters into their hands and give you some input on how the advertisement should look or who they think they should be targeting. This is the wrong approach on their end because they should know they aren't the expert here — you are. However, we deal with clients like this in the beginning because they are sometimes the only revenue we can find before we build up enough of a portfolio to fire them.

If you decided to keep the physical therapist in the dark regarding how you're delivering leads from the very beginning, they'll have no opportunity to come at you and give their input on how the ad should look because they don't even know what the ad looks like, to begin with. This is a healthy relationship between client and agency. The client having only a very small hand in the process and the agency doing all the work — this is exactly why the agency was hired, after all.

The thing to keep in mind when selling your digital services is that you're not selling the actual services. These are merely a means to generate more leads — you are selling branding, brand awareness, an online presence, and lead generation. All of the facets that are involved in generating an online presence increase the bottom line and push the needle in the right direction because you're eventually using that leverage to generate leads. Selling *brand awareness* is especially difficult because there's no direct return on it. You have to demonstrate the value of what having a large Facebook following with have for the client, then sell that.

You may come across some clients who are so out of touch and left in the dark that they are unaware of the internet nearly as a whole, to begin with. These prospects aren't immediately lost causes but they're damned close. The minute you find yourself describing the most basic benefits of the internet is when you have to put on your more aggressive sales hat and tell them how they're missing out big time by not investing in this. This is going to be difficult for some business owners to stomach because they usually will be invested in their strategy — whatever it is — and be less willing to take the new approach that you are selling them.

An example of this is real estate agents who swear by their direct mail marketing. Traditional direct mail is not dead, but it is certainly not as effective as digital marketing. Propose to people like this that you can take that exact same budget and produce double the amount of leads by reaching 10x the amount of people. Between printing and postage, you could virtually touch exponentially more people using online advertising. Proposing this value will be the challenge and that will rely heavily on your sales approach and your sales tactics.

Lead generation is easy because it'll be very transactional — you can choose to charge clients based on leads you're bringing in or charge them a retainer for building and maintaining the platform in which they will be generating leads.

So long as your clients are getting enough leads that convert to sales and those sales cover your cost, they should be satisfied for a bit. The goal, of course, will be that these marketing services exponentially improve their bottom line — which it will, just not the first month!

Brand awareness is tricky because it's not very quantifiable — what are their goals? Drive more traffic to their website? Drive likes and video views on their Facebook pages?

Always remember, facebook likes provide very little value besides outside of the company's vanity. You don't get any money from a like nor is it even a lead. However, getting a brand out there and building popularity will naturally drive more traffic and sales — these metrics are very difficult to put a value on. Determining a worth your client will happily pay will be the struggle here.

Content creation is nice because it involves deliverables — you can produce video content for them, ask them to prepare a script (or you can offer PR services and include the script for them) or you can produce blog posts and copywriting — all which will drive traffic but that's not what you're selling.

The transaction that involves one item that everyone agreed on is easy to make quick one-time payments. A 15-page website, a 2,000-word blog post, or a 5-minute commercial are all understood by each party and there's no relying on advertisements.

Establish your online presence

Eat your own dogfood — this means you do exactly what you would do for your clients to yourself. This will show that you have the ability and are willing to put in the energy to build other businesses just as you are your own.

Establishing authority is crucial. No one is going to trust some Joe Doe off the street unless you can prove that you know what you're talking about.

LinkedIn is where so many of your prospects are going to live. If you can establish some likes and shares on LinkedIn, you will easily have some steady leads knocking on your email asking to work with you. This is where the professionals hang out and it'll really benefit you if you can be respected on this platform.

When Calaboration was in the early stages, people weren't buying our story 100%. At networking events during our initial pitches, they'd hear us out and essentially think to themselves that they're not going to work with us. Sure enough, someone I thought I had lost calls me up the next day and says, "Nick — I was browsing your website and I did not realize you were so legit."

This conversation turned into a deal with him and two other people connected to him. This is all because he perceived us as a premium and established agency from the website. This is marketing and eating your own dogfood will allow you to do this as well.

Week One: Step By Step

1. **Finding your value**.
   Sit down and think about where you can add value. Are you familiar with the medical industry? Maybe you can target physical therapists, massage parlors, or nail salons. Whatever it is, just pick something and you can always tweak it later. Now that you know what you can target, research it.
   Simply search: `<INDUSTRY> digital marketing. See what the state of the market is for that industry and those services. Do your due diligence.`
2. **Learn the benefit of services you want to provide**.
   I'm not even asking you to learn the ins and outs of Facebook marketing yet. I'm only suggesting that you learn enough about it to be able to sell it. You want to be able to go into a company, tell them the benefits, impacts, and effects this marketing strategy can have on their business. You don't need to know how to do it to be able to sell them on it.
3. **Observe how others are doing it**.
   You're not the first person to do digital marketing for a real estate agent or a local pub. There is information out there on how to provide leads and marketing for whatever niche you

decide on. Read some blog posts and understand how you can help these specific industries.
4. **Start the website**.
I have the website so early in this process because it's going to be the place that all roads lead to. When you're speaking in person to a prospect or blasting some tweets about your business, this is where people are going to see some work you've done (it's ok you have none) and an email address to get in touch with. If absolutely nothing else, this also gives you the ability to form an email address which is the next thing we're going to talk about.
5. **Create your agency email**.
This is more difficult than it has any right to be but you can get it done in a matter of minutes if you know where to look. This is a very important step in this process because, like the website being where all roads lead to, the email is where everyone at the website is going to go next. Nothing is worse than having an `@gmail address and it will immediately out you as a beginner who has never worked with a business before (even though you might not have)`.
6. **Further establish your online presence**.
Now that you're taken seriously with a website and email address, it's time to put those to work and start putting yourself out there so you can let the world know you're ready to take on new clients (or first clients).
You can do this by posting some insights on Facebook, Twitter, or even by ranting on youtube here and there. Anything online is going to drive *some* traffic even if it's very very little.
7. **Rest and refine**.
Take a step back and ensure everything is in order. Check to make sure the email is working — send some test emails. Make sure the website is looking good on mobile devices as well as tablets and desktops, and plan out some blog posts or videos to start building your online presence a little — remember, you're not aiming for global traffic here. You just want some little things to share with prospects so they can

see you're active in the community and know what you're actually talking about.

Get to Work

You've managed to take the first steps to creat your digital agency. These are somewhat boring and menial tasks that just had to get done. You need the website, you need the email, and you need some of these groundwork things in order before you can start injecting yourself into the market.

Week Two: Entering the Market

[Before you actually enter the market](#) you need to know what you're entering with.

Figuring out what the value you're providing is one thing, productizing your services, finding the people who will want to buy them, and selling is a whole other thing.

As soon as you start your agency, you should be [focusing on finding clients](#). [Networking](#), scraping the web for emails, and marketing yourself is going to be the best ways you can go about this at first. Next, you'll want to sort out your products and/or services and figure out how you can most effectively sell packages that might fit anyone and everyone's business.

Sell Results

Since you're likely working on a digital marketing agency, examples of your *products* might be Facebook advertising services, blogging, and other content strategies. This means you build out the ad campaigns, posts, engagement, and whatever else you feel you should include in that product.

The *result* of this product is that they have a maintained Facebook page, constant updates to their websites, and an overall responsive web presence. You're not *selling* the Facebook management, you're selling the ramifications of the managed Facebook presence — this is part of your product's package.

Facebook ads and Google Adwords is another product that you can serve that will allow your users to have ads running on multiple platforms thus diversifying their reach.

[The service is you building out these ads and curating the audiences and their result is covering more ground and generating leads through multiple channels](#).

Google Adwords and SEO is another service you could consider. Once you move from advertising to other services you can give them a taste of what else you can do. SEO falls under digital marketing but is technically a separate service. now you have to determine what your SEO services are — you have to *productize* your SEO services and determine the *results* you're selling.

There are so many things you can do with SEO and it's important to actually determine what you're going to be doing so they're not caught off guard. We find many people selling ripoff SEO services that don't actually do anything at all.

Their results may be: *"get me on the front page of google".*

If this is the case, if they're willing to dump all the money in the world for you to accomplish that by any means necessary, great, take it. but some companies won't be so willing and will need actual deliverables.

1. 2 blog posts per month + keywords research will involve you actually giving them blog posts and optimizing their site for keywords.
2. 4 blog posts per month, link building, and local business indexing is another one.
3. Even 8 blog posts per month is a viable SEO strategy.

Start Selling

Once you're aware of what you're going to be selling you have to actually get out there and start selling it.

There are many ways you can win clients

- Knowing people
- Networking
- Your own online presence and SEO
- Referrals

These are all great to have and you will get them after even only landing one client to show off your work.

Perceived value is when you go in and make them so pumped for your services that they see nothing but value and they are astonished at the rate you're giving them. *Actual* value of whatever you're doing is less important than the *percieved* value — make people believe you're worth your premium prices and they'll happily pay it.

If they think it's too expensive, they don't perceive the value correctly — that's your fault. If they think they don't need certain services or packages, they don't perceive the value — again, your fault.

Getting them to understand the value is going to be the hardest part here because they may want to see results first or simply don't trust you to deliver on your promises — do not work for free and just refine your sales approach so they can sign on the dotted line.

[Reputation](). Unfortunately, there's not much you can do here if you're just starting out. No one is going to refer you or vouch for you if you haven't done any work for anyone yet.

However, your [reputation]() can rely on other facets of your being than just your previous work.

> I was [at a networking event with a prospect]() I've met with a couple times. We haven't signed anything and it wasn't looking too promising as far as aligning an agreement that would work for both of us — however, we were very friendly and happy to continue discussing it even at this networking event. Later in the event, we stroll around together meeting other business owners and he's touting Calaboration as the best marketing firm in the venue and that he uses us — he doesn't even use us! This was him simply giving us good reviews in the open so we can make a better impression on everyone. [This goes to show you can build a *brand* and *reputation* without actually doing any work]()!

Sales ability: This is the one thing that you have complete control over and can refine to such a degree that no matter who you're in the room with you can sell them. Your sales skills are going to be exponentially more valuable than your actual technical ability once you land these clients. Even the smallest amount of work that monkeys can do can bring companies so much value and it's your job to sell them on that idea before they even have any leads coming through.

How you sell is going to play a massive role in how you run your business and [what types of clients you get](). **Clients are the only thing that matter to your business** since nothing else differentiates you from the top agencies except that you're landing local real estate agents and they're landing fortune 50 companies.

A good salesperson can sell a product no matter how good or bad it may be. This is crucial to master because you don't even really *have* a product to sell just yet. You have fairy dust that you're going to figure out how to turn into results later on.

Productizing

[Maximizing your efficiency in the office and in your business](#) is helpful when you're a CEO wearing many different hats. Productizing your services increases your efficiency and effectiveness because your packages are already sorted out and can be more off-the-shelf.

Productizing is a highly productive practice since it, effectively, automates some of the sales processes. Instead of packaging together a complex and bespoke option for each client, you can figure out what everyone needs and fit it all in one service. This is how you can produce systems and eventually automate these systems so they can get done in a timely fashion. Operations and automation can turn your business around.

Once you build out *products* that you can then sell, you'll have a clearer idea of what you're selling and how you can help.

You know exactly how to help certain industries with specific problems. The good news is that once you've done your market research and determined that a few professionals are having the same exact problem, you can cut out so much work by productizing your services. This means that you create a single *package* of services that you can put a price tag on and sell in bulk. You'll cut down your consultation time since you've done this before and you can charge a premium — again — since you've done this before.

Productization is the best way to begin scaling since it will allow you to get more done, in less time, and with more clients. Many prospects won't know what they want. They may have heard that digital advertising works but it's completely foreign to them. They may have been meaning to get their email newsletter launched but they have no patience to actually pull the trigger. When you come in and say that you've worked with similar businesses with similar problems and solved it with this one strategy, they'll be delighted to know there's no guesswork on your end and that their bottom line will grow as a result of your services.

You'll find it difficult to create a scalable package early on since you have to speak to many business professionals and gain intel before you know what the priorities they're all struggling with are. If you've spoken with ten real estate agents and they all tell you they have trouble filming their listings and getting that out to Facebook and YouTube, this is clearly a priority that people are having trouble actually implementing. Now, with this new knowledge, you know you can easily get away with telling future prospects that you handle this as part of the package you're offering. They'll be happy to see that you understand their problems even before they've explained them to you.

Creating tiers and packages like this helps your agency grow as well. You're now able to sell a clearly defined package that you've templated and can sell and sell over and over again instead of spending weeks coming to a perfect and bespoke strategy for one unique client. Since you've created processes and templates for these services, you know exactly how to take action once they sign on as a client and you're merely going through motions that you've done time and time again. If you're thinking like a true agency owner, you'll see where we're going next with this.

How to Find Clients

Now that you know how to win the businesses, you need to know where to find them.

You're going to learn that there are no great spots to find clients, many terrible spots to find clients and that [you'll find amazing clients totally unexpectedly based on connections alone](#).

> We were in a big lunch meeting one time with someone looking for a large website deal along with some services to go along with it. Everything was going well. After lunch, we head back to the office and in the elevator run into one of his friends who runs another business in the same building. He told him what we do and he expresses

how he's in the market for digital services — we ended up closing a deal with his friend before we ever did with the other prospect we were there for!

Walking your local main street is the easiest way to find some local businesses that you can easily help. They're probably run by a generation who have never even thought of doing any type of digital marketing — this is great because it gives you a perfect opportunity to sell them on the idea *and* you can provide so much value off the bat since they will be starting from scratch.

Check out local chamber of commerce and business related meetups where you can find like-minded business owners that you can then start pitching to.

You can easily find conferences, events, and other things that are specific to a certain industry. Where are all the dentists hanging out if you are specializing in that? Every single person there would then be a potential client.

Go to real estate investor groups (there are tons) if you're targeting that demographic as well — again, every single person there will need your services and **since it's not a marketing meetup and instead are meetup you may be the only one there**.

Business listing sites are where we're actually going to start because you can literally begin right now. You don't have to register for any events, accounts, or memberships. You can actually start reaching out to businesses right now using some sites like yellow pages yellow book and yelp.

There are a few approaches you can take from here are we're going to talk about them next.

How to Reach Out to Prospects

Cold calling

Cold calling is not dead. Anyone who tells you it is is too lazy or scared to do it themselves so they don't want anyone else doing it.

Go through local businesses, look at their websites and understand what they're selling. Then, immediately go in for the call — spend too much time prequalifying and thinking and you'll talk yourself out of the call altogether.

Here's your step by step regarding cold calling

1. Speak confidently and clearly
2. Make them like you
3. Express interest in their company
4. [Set up the meeting](#)

This should be your only goal while on this call — to get in the door and speak to them one on one in person. once you're here, your sales skills will come in handy and you'll land clients.

Some **common objections** you can handle right then and there while in the cold call are:

1. **What do you charge?**
   This isn't even so much an objection since they're showing some type of interest. the truth is, you don't want to work with someone who's interested in cost before you even had a conversation. Doctors don't prescribe medications before you came to an appointment, just like you can't give a quote on services you don't even know yet until you meet with them.

   Say something like, "we have a range of services starting at $1000/mo with some clients on our $8 or $10,000/mo plan. They always see a return within the first three months.
2. **We don't need marketing.**
   This is harsh and you should question their business. Some businesses truly don't need marketing if their product is so good and viral that everyone does marketing for them for free. The truth is, if a local pizzeria doesn't have a Facebook page, they're leaving money on the table. That alone is something easy enough for you to do and low-budget enough for them to justify.
3. **We've been burned in the past.**
   This is unfortunately true (and common). Since so many individuals call themselves digital marketers, they think they can build out a site and run some ads and eventually fail at it

and give up. This will require top-notch sales ability since you're now forced to prove your legitimacy over the phone.

Ultimately, getting on the phone is going to put you over most digital marketers out there bc so many of them just communicate on Facebook and email. business owners like seeing other hungry entrepreneurs pitch them and will respect you. Never apologize for bothering anyone on the phone and never feel like you're pestering them by following up aggressively.

> We once landed a client after only one call and one meeting. He said to me, "Nick, you're actually here. You showed up to the office in the snow and are pitching me this marketing which you clearly know very well. I know I want to work with someone like this since the majority of people pitching me similar things are too afraid to even get on the phone".

Showing up and being human will differentiate you.

Cold Emailing

Cold emailing, though less powerful than calling, can be just as effective because you can send out 2000 emails in the time it takes you to make one call.

You can effectively accumulate 200 emails of local businesses, bars, and real estate agents and blast out the same email to all of them.

Once some of them reply, they're warm leads to follow up with a call and they'll already be expecting to get pitched.

Here are some examples of effective cold emails:

> Hey <name>,
> I noticed your latest listing in <city> near my hometown — love the listing.
> I actually help other agents in the area get more listings like that through digital marketing.
> Is <phone> still the best number to reach you?
> Thanks and talk soon!

Nick

You can mail merge and put in more information like listings if they're a real estate agent, recent projects if they're a construction company, and even areas of interest that they do business in so they know you're giving them the most personal email possible.

Networking

Digital marketing is a commoditized service. What this means for you is that you have to really stand out and prove to people why they'd work for you over someone else offering the same services. As we've said above, anyone can build a website — you're the special feature people are paying for.

Much like plumbers, [real estate agents, mortgage lenders](), HVAC professionals, and many, many more professions, digital marketers are everywhere and they're always looking for work. In the same fashion electricians are constantly attending networking events and keeping themselves relevant looking for their next job, digital marketers do the same thing.

When starting out, physically networking may be the greatest asset to your business compared to every other method of obtaining clients. Networking events and meetups will put you in front of the people who are willing and able to buy from you — be present and turn on the charm to [get more work for your digital agency]().

Why [Networking](#) is so Effective For Your Digital Agency

Websites are websites — at the end of the day, it rarely matters who *built* it and many businesspeople would have a difficult time deciphering the difference between something you build and something your competitor down the block built. Unfortunately, this means who clients buy digital marketing from is a lot less logical than it should be. Fortunately, this means there's an opportunity to be exploited.

Imagine you and your competitor can build the same exact website using the same tools — neither is better nor worse than the other. Which agency is this law firm in need of a web presence going to hire? Let's take a look at their options and how they might approach this.

First, a lawyer might reach out to their network and ask if anyone knows anybody — the opportunity is already there because whoever this person is asking could easily have done work with you in the past and recommend you. If you're in that referral circle you're off to a great start — you probably got into that referral circle by meeting their acquaintances at a networking event. You met them in person at some point.

If the lawyer still struggles to find someone after their network wasn't able to provide any names, they resort to *their* networking. Perhaps they're going to a business cocktail hour — you better believe they'll be on the lookout for some marketing people.

At the cocktail hour, the lawyer meets Joe from *Joe's Media & Marketing*. Joe and the lawyer speak a bit since they can both help each other out professionally. The lawyer is impressed with the work Joe's done and takes his business card for later use — it seems likely this lawyer might be setting up a meeting with Joe's Media & Marketing to get some deals moving!

Later that night, the lawyer runs into you. Although the lawyer already has someone in mind for their website, they're always eager to network, meet new professionals, and possibly weigh some options and have someone bid for their work. You and the lawyer are connecting really well and they're a big fan of your charm and wit. You barely even talk about your experience but they get the idea that you're more than qualified to handle their website and such.

The next day, the lawyer forgot all about Joe's Media & Marketing and calls you immediately. They want to set up a time to talk more details and get a website up and running! You have this job in the bag — the lawyer is happy to give the work to you because they like you as a person as well as a businessperson. Truthfully, Joe might have been the better option, he's done law sites in the past, he's older, and maybe he's even more professional — but the lawyer really liked you and your personality so they decided it's better to give the work to you since they'll be more comfortable with **you**.

Notice how much revolves around you — [you are the differentiating factor](#) between all digital marketing agencies. You are why someone is going to choose your firm over someone else's.

How Networking Has Helped [My Digital Agency](#)

When I first started Calaboration, I did nothing but attend business meetups, breakfasts, lunches, dinners, and happy hours. I wanted to encounter every single person who considered themselves a business. Everyone needs a website — if you didn't have one I was in your face pitching you one.

This may seem aggressive — but it worked. Being aware of my strengths, I was always able to determine how I could most easily get a new deal. I found I was most appealing and made most contacts in crowds, whether speaking in front of them or mingling within them. By understanding that speaking, gesticulating, and entertaining people in the real world would be my greatest shot of getting initial work, I immersed myself in all the networking events I possibly could've.

I quickly became friends with some of the top real estate agents and lenders in the state. Although I didn't get much work from them in particular, they're so well-connected they're always happy to throw me some names of people who need websites.

This wasn't something that I was able to do very well while others were unable to. This was just being present. Woody Allen says, "80 percent of life is showing up" — this goes to show that you could be stumbling on your words, wearing unprofessional clothing, and anything else that would seemingly ruin your chances and still get the job; all because you showed up.

Of course, we suggest learning all you can about proper conversational skills and such, but the big picture is that by showing up and being in front of these people, you already have a huge edge and beat out 80% of the competition since they couldn't make it out that day.

"80 percent of life is showing up" ~ Woody Allen

Don't get discouraged when you go to a few events and meet the same people who aren't giving you work. This is just like building a brand and will take time — you may get lucky and land a client after your first day out, or it could take a month for you to build the necessary relationships that'll result in a new client — whatever it is it is crucial to continue on and persevere.

Ultimately, if you want to get clients quickly and are willing to put in the legwork, networking events could be extremely resourceful. Getting out of bed at 6 am for early breakfast networking and staying out until 10 for cocktail events will not be sustainable forever. Go out and do it now so you can build the foundation for your digital agency.

How to Network to Get Clients

Networking is a skill like any other. It can be acquired, refined, and even perfected. It goes on for a while and takes a lot of time to *win* at networking. Just like branding, networking is building a reputation and using it to win you more trust and more work.

You walk into a happy hour and everyone is wearing a sports coat and holding their gin and tonics. You pay your $20 admission fee and start walking around. Where do you begin?

Nail Your Pitch

How are you introducing yourself?

> Hello all, I'm Nick Calabro with Calaboration — a digital marketing and media agency. We've worked with politicians and real estate agents to build their websites, execute lead generation tactics, and even their more traditional marketing desires. Thanks for putting on the event and I look forward to meeting you all!

If an event calls for everyone going around the room, you should craft a short bio of yourself and your company that you can always repeat. Say this with more confidence than anything you've ever said.

Find People in Groups of Three

You don't normally want to barrel into a conversation between just two people. They're likely engaged in each other and don't really have room to let you in. This is why it's best to find a group of three people or more — the natural progression of conversations will eventually favor two people and there will be somebody slightly left out; this is who you can pursue a conversation with since they'll be yearning for someone to speak to them anyway.

The Approach

Find a group and walk up to it — I wish I could say there was more to it.

Typically, people will welcome you into their circle. You can introduce yourself, give your little pitch, and ask what everyone else does. When you find someone that has something in common with you or that you want to learn more about, simply shift over to them and ask for their card. This will spark a conversation and you're networking!

Talk to the Right People

You never want to avoid anyone — everyone and anyone would be great contacts for you and could always have the potential to help you out in the future. With that said, you are there to get business. If you're selling digital marketing and web design, you probably don't want to be talking to all the other digital marketers at the event. In fact, you want to make rounds as soon as possible so you can get in front of people before they can.

Don't Get Trapped

If you find yourself getting wrapped up in boring conversations that are all about the other person and have no chance of leading to anything valuable for you, you have every right to bail. Your business is the most important one at that event, don't harm your lead pipeline because you wanted to be polite and listen to someone tell stories about their grandchildren.

Speak Loudly & Confidently

I consider myself very lucky that I naturally speak loudly and exude excitement. People tell me all the time how they appreciate my passion and hunger — I look at them oddly because this is my effortless state, but it's increasingly becoming clear that these are some of the traits that are *neccesary* to succeed at networking.

People will always remember the person that made them feel good, that made them laugh, and that showed they were happy to be in their presence. No one is going to remember the person that says, "I guess I can fix your toilet" in a monotonous tone.

Business Cards

I'm sure as soon as you decided on a name for your agency you designed some business cards. It's a very entertaining process to go through because it's a tangible reward for your efforts of becoming an agency CEO.

Networking events probably account for 90% of the business card printing industry. You will receive hundreds and you'll give out thousands. I hardly meet anyone that doesn't get a copy of my business card and I try to get one from everyone I meet.

The secret to this business is being in front of people. When you have jacket pocket full of business cards, send out emails to each one of those the next morning.

> Hi Barb, great meeting you last night. It was great getting some insights into your industry and I'm eager to learn more about this. I'd love to buy you a coffee or get together in some capacity so we can talk more about your business and if there's anything we can do to work together.
>
> Calaboration has worked with other accounting firms in the past and I'd love to get a feel for how you're currently doing it.

Thanks so much and talk soon!
Nick

Where to Network for Digital Marketing Clients

At first, it is going to seem like there are so many networking events and that you'll never be able to go to them all. Soon, after you go to all of them, you'll learn that only a few out of those thirty were any good. You might stick to a certain couple that you're happy with and attend those weekly and be done with it.

The different types of groups will keep you busy throughout the day as well. Morning breakfast groups usually start very early and will take up about 90-120 minutes. Afternoon lunch clubs will have a different vibe but ultimately offer the same thing. Things get different when you're dealing in happy hour and have to navigate the bar and everyone standing around.

[BNI](#) — Business Networking Company is a very popular networking group that you can find anywhere. There are probably a few chapters near your area that you can test out and find one that fits.

[LeTip](#) — Much like BNI, LeTip is a referral network. You sit in a circle, give a speech about what you do and who your clients are, and sit back down. You're encouraged (and sometimes forced) to bring referrals for someone else in the group so you can all have a powerful pipeline.

One thing to keep in mind with groups like BNI and LeTip is that they don't allow anyone joining who might be a competitor to someone already in the group. They're very strict about having one person from the industry only at each group. This allows the system of passing referrals to work so well — as soon as I learn my neighbor needs a plumber, I'm going directly to my designated plumber at the group instead of choosing someone out of a pool.

[Meetup](#) — Just doing a quick search on Meetup.com for business events will bring up many options. These are going to be less structured since there's (likely) no big company behind them, but they will make for great experiences.

After Networking

Like we stated above, the best thing you can do after a networking event is reaching out to everyone. Hopefully, you listened and garnered enough data at the event to coherently have a conversation later on with them as well.

Meet for coffee, help them with their social media, and build that brand. You're going to be a friend to them forever now and even though most of them will never return favors and help you out, the ones that do will make it so worth it. Happy networking.

Week Two: Step by Step

1. **Write out your products**
   Get some pen and paper and draw out 3 or 4 productized services you can provide with clear results that you'll be selling.
2. **Aggregate emails**
   This process will take you longer than you think. You can always buy leads but that isn't recommended just yet since

you want to at least land one client so you're not breaking the bank and you can sustain the business.

look through local MLSs, yellow pages, and other resources that will have emails and phone numbers. Keep them all in one spreadsheet with partitioned email, company name, first and last name, phone number, and the channel you found them on.

3. **Email blasts**

   This is when you take your database of 50, 100, or more emails and finally craft your personalized email merge to them all.

   Download some email software and go to town.

4. **Start cold calling**

   The best time to cold call will be around lunchtime or late afternoon. If you're working a full-time job this might be tough which is why we have multiple avenues like email as well. However, even if you call after work, say at 5 pm or even anytime before 8 pm, you will have a pretty good shot at catching business owners since their lives are their businesses and they will likely be working longer hours than just the typical office hours.

5. **Repeat getting emails and sending out emails**

   Ideally, you want to send out new emails to new sets of contacts every day. This might not be viable since the aggregation process will take so long, but do it whenever you find a spare minute.

6. **Repeat cold calling and follow up**

   By later in the week you should have some email responses and interested people from your cold calling campaign. This is the perfect time to allocate some resources and follow up with them through email, calling up prospects that emails you back, and cultivating these contacts to bring them to a sale.

7. **Refine**

   You're going to want to take a day and look back at how you're doing and figure things out. This is going to be valuable so you can ensure you're not missing people calling you back or emailing you without your knowledge.

The worst thing that can happen to a sale is time. let too

much time pass and they'll forget about you and you'll never close.

Week Three: How to Sell Your Digital Marketing Services

Your products, services, and overall company is nothing unless you can sell. Do you know why salespeople get treated like kings and queens at companies? Because, if it weren't for them, the company would be no company at all. They drive the revenue; they make things happen — you have to (initially) make things happen.

You will have no trouble selling digital marketing services in today's market since there are many more businesses sprouting up that need marketing than not. Creating perceived value is critical to easily get clients to hand over money to you and your agency — have them believe you're worth what you're saying and you will always sell your digital marketing services.

Selling

Your services are nothing if you fail to invite people to them and hold their hand through the process of going from lead to closed client. The sales process required for a digital agency like yours will include a pipeline with a structure like: Lead, initial touch, meeting, proposal, negotiation, close — win/lose.

Every single person you meet should go in the lead portion of your pipeline. It won't be hard to determine if they're qualified immediately and if you should invest any time in pursuing them. Once you reach out to your leads, give a quick pitch to what it is your agency does, and attempt to set up a meeting, you will record how that initial touch went in your CRM so you can refer back to what was said and if they dropped any hints as to [what they might want in their proposal](), should they receive one down the line.

Preparing for this initial meeting shouldn't be too daunting. You're merely grabbing a coffee or visiting them at their office. As far as they should be able to tell, you're not yet selling them on anything. This is beneficial for them and for you because it puts them in a more comfortable frame of mind and it prevents you from getting bent out of shape if you're nervous about the sales process. Since we're only meeting and greeting, there is absolutely no pressure.

Like a perfect match on a first date, this meeting can very quickly turn into something more and heat up in a matter of minutes. The second you hear them describe how they're unhappy with their current supplier of digital services is your cue to jump in and start qualifying.

> How are you currently getting your leads?
> Do you have an email list that you keep in contact with?
> Do you drive any paid traffic to your website currently?

These are all great questions that will get the prospect thinking in terms of what they're not doing and what you can potentially provide since you're the one getting them to consider it at all. If their answers are anything that isn't completely shooting down what you're saying — you have a solid shot at making this sale. At this point, they're a red-hot qualified lead; don't mess it up.

Casually mention how all the problems that they're struggling with are things that your agency actually works on with existing clients.

> You mention that you don't email your list as often as you'd like — we actually manage some clients' email lists and maintain their email marketing strategies for them; it's included in the marketing package they have with us.

You've now opened up the floor for them to dig more into what it is that you provide and how you can help them. Get in there and describe your services and how they can help your client. More importantly — remember — focus on the results that these services provide.

> By sending out weekly email blasts to their contact list of over 20,000, they get at least 100 responses of interested buyers every time an email goes out. More importantly, the rest of the people with our open rate of nearly 50% are constantly reminded of the client and what they do so they're always top of mind.

This is a solid pitch for email marketing because you're proposing multiple streams of potential value with technically only one service. Email marketing is providing [brand awareness](), lead generation, and constant contact with their potential buyers. You're not telling them about the software you're using to blast out the emails or the layouts you're using to generate the funnel pages — you're simply giving them the overall tool that is used to get them the results that increase their bottom line.

Once you talk about all you can do and the benefits of everything, ask if they have a marketing budget and what they're looking to spend on this. We'll go into tactics to hit them with if they're pushing back on your prices in later programs but for right now laying down on your first client isn't the worst thing that has happened to an early agency owner. Explain to them that you'll write something up for them and be in touch very shortly.

The minute you leave their vicinity [you should begin writing up their proposal](). Give a detailed description of what you're doing to do, what benefits they can see, and cater it extremely specifically to their unique situation and business. This will give them a sense that you understand their industry and their issues and that you are more fit than anyone else to serve them because competing agencies handed them a templated proposal that is generic enough to be handed to just about any business owner in any market.

As soon as you shoot them the write-up, give a call and follow up so you can walk through the proposal together and there's no ambiguity regarding your services, their expectations, and your pricing. Send over a payable-by-credit card invoice and begin building a foundation for your first client.

How to Sell

> "Outstanding people have one thing in common: An absolute sense of mission." ~ Zig Ziglar

You have to always be working. Everyone in real estate says things along the lines of, "No matter where I am or what I'm doing, I want everyone to know I'll sell their house or sell them a house."

That is absolute and true devotion to the mission and this has to be you if you hope to sell more digital marketing services. If you're at the ice cream parlor with your kids and see they have a poor Facebook page, you have to take some initiative and say to the manager that you can help them drive more traffic and increase sales.

You have to be aggressive with follow up as well. You must be shameless when it comes to rejection and you have to believe in yourself and your product too heavily that these things come so easily and naturally to you.

You'll find people appreciate your seemingly severe outreach instead of being annoyed by it. Buyers rarely want to take initiative and hand someone a fat check for digital services that they can't even tangibly handle — this doesn't mean that they do not want it and it certainly doesn't mean that they do not need it. The art of sales is knowing how to hold someone's hand through their entire buying process and removing all effort and friction from them so that all they have to do is sign on the dotted line and start directly depositing your money.

Your CRM and pipeline

Your CRM is your customer relationship manager — this is where all your leads go and how you keep track of where accounts are in the sales process and what your next actions on them are. You'll be including things such as leads, their info, important dates, organizations, and more.

Incoming Leads: This is how you can ensure that everyone you come in contact with is going to get pitched eventually and somehow. This is the way you want it to be. Everyone starts off as a lead and you disqualify from there.

Since digital services are so broad and widely desired, nearly every person you encounter from plumbers to hotel managers could do business with you. Because of this, your pipeline should be extremely full as opposed to enterprise SaaS products' sales teams' who may only have 1000 buyers in the entire country.

Contact Info: This is important because even those that you're not directly doing business with can be great contacts. You want to keep their birthdays, special events they tell you about so you can be reminded about them later on, and other things like that in your CRM so you're always on top of the people that matter most to you and your business.

Your pipeline is one of the most important things to your business. You want to keep your pipeline full and always moving to the right (toward the close column). You're going to walk prospects through your sales process delicately and eventually close the sale — whether that closing is a win or lose. Keep in mind, losing deals is fine if you're losing them in a timely fashion. Get people to say *no* during the first meeting instead of five meetings and three months down the line when you've invested time and energy into them.

Your CRM is also useful to track how certain projects for specific accounts are going. Since your CRM is, hopefully, cloud-based and everyone on the team has access to it, you can easily collaborate and ensure everyone's on the same track regarding one accounts' website and another's video production.

Organizations: You'll find many CRMs do a great (and sometimes confusing) job at partitioning between the individual, organization, type of lead, and so many other parameters. This is good and bad: bad because it may be confusing at first, but good for literally every other reason. You want to ensure that you aren't pitching to the wrong person, going over someone's head, or someone that doesn't like the other person in the same company — it may sound absurd, but never forget that you're dealing with people, not logical computer programs or robots, people with feelings. By tracking which companies you're pitching to, the actual person, their role, and their history, you'll have a much better idea of how to close the sale.

Collaboration: Like we mentioned before, your CRM should be in the cloud. Don't be foolish and ensure your connections are always secure and such since this is extremely sensitive information. [Once you claim a client](#), everyone on the sales team should understand and respect that they're yours. Similarly, if you lost a client, everyone needs to know that in case someone planned on doing something with the account later on.

Dates & Misc. Info: Your CRM should act as your second mind and secretary. Instead of having an intern follow you around during parties giving you factoids on who is who, you can always whip out your CRM's mobile application and do enough due diligence to intelligently speak to somebody.

Great CRM's have data from years in the past that have been organized and cultivated for a while. This is great for you if you're enjoying all the free information, but somebody had to create that system in the first place. Be the one for your agency to add all the important and personable information so your future salesforce will effectively take over.

Pipeline

Since you should consider anyone and everyone a lead no matter what, how can we properly manage them all in our pipeline? Put them through your sales process and if they have other qualifications or can be useful somewhere else just put them where they belong in whichever pipeline is best at the time.

You may have separate pipelines for a video production project than you do for a website project. You may have certain prospects in multiple pipelines at once. Whatever the individual case calls for, it's important to organize everyone where they belong so contacts don't fall through the cracks — there's nothing worse than losing a deal because you failed to follow up.

Next is prospecting. That person you met at the bar who gave you their business card to stay in touch is only a lead. You know nothing about them. Prospecting is getting leads that would be ever so slightly more valuable — you probably wouldn't actively go to the bar to prospect and generate leads unless you were selling booze or cigarettes. This is when you send emails to only those that are working in the medical field, or only going to real estate meetups, for example. You're prospecting because you're hitting the people that have a higher potential of doing business with you. You're cutting out the fat and intentionally putting yourself in the environment that your perfect lead hangs out in.

This can be especially difficult if you don't know where your perfect lead *hangs out*. Calaborationdoes work for municipalities and politicians. It's not always intuitive where to find a list of every public figure running for office — it's always easy to find a group of real estate agents. Finding where your ideal client hangs out is crucial to how full your pipeline remains.

Qualifying can be done during the first meeting or even the first phone call or email. This is when you ask them the questions that would indicate if they'd be interested in and willing to take action on your services. Ask things like:

- What's your budget?
- Are you working with other agencies at the moment?
- What's your timeline?

All these contribute to your next step which is determining their needs.

Needs Analysis. Here, you are in the meeting and figuring out exactly how you can work together. You're deciding on timelines together and hashing out details about how it may look if you all move forward. If this all goes well and everyone is comfortable with pricing and timing, then you can send over the proposal.

You never want anyone to be surprised when they get the proposal. Include all the nitty-gritty details and such and ensure you don't sticker shock them with pricing that wasn't discussed earlier. This should be done a week, at maximum, after your needs analysis meeting. Obviously, offer to come in or hop on a call so you can walk through the proposal together and not have them sitting there wondering what you're actually going to be doing for them.

Negotiation. They will likely come back at you with some requests to change and remove some things. This is perfectly fine but ensure you're not taking any losses.

An early Calaboration client's agreement came out to just about over $2,000 per month. The exact figure was an odd number that only came out that way because it was such a custom package. There were too many negotiations we eventually pulled the agreement altogether.

The prospect firstly wanted to bring the cost down to an even number which was oddly annoying because this delayed the entire process an extra week so they can save a couple hundred dollars. This was a red flag immediately because if someone is going to cause a fuss over that kind of savings they will likely not be a fun client to work with.

Further, negotiations cost you money. You're not only losing money by bringing down the price for this prospect, but you're actively rewriting proposals and scheduling more meetings to go over revisions. After three negotiating meetings, that deal is dead and no longer worth it.

Close. Finally, you're there. If you made it this far and still lost the client, eat the time and energy wasted and put it away as a learning experience. Cut your deadweight prospects before you make it this far by aggressively selling and getting them to say no early and often — this will save you hundreds of hours.

If you won the client, congratulations! Now get to work.

Sales Process and Follow Up

You're going to start with the [initial meeting](). This is where you get introduced via email, cold call, or at an event. You're both very cold but it's your job to warm them up and get them to do business with you.

You always want to follow up with your leads and prospects.

Like we mentioned earlier, you should always stay on top of people until they tell you no. Even when they tell you no, you want to reach back out to them in a few months once their situation has changed.

You want to email them right away after you receive their business card for the first time. If no answer, you want to hit them again a week later. If it's someone you really want, you would even give a call and even drop by.

Process

Here is the typical process we take at [Calaboriton](). It can be refined and if you're a master salesperson you would get this all done in one step but we're not all Zig Ziglar.

Set up a meeting. I don't care who it is or what they do but just get in front of them. If absolutely nothing else, you'll be able to ask them who they know who may need you.

During this meeting, you'll be doing one of two things. They're either expecting a pitch and want you to tell them more about what you do, or they'll just be [networking](). Come ready to sell and give the presentation. This is where you figure out what deck you'll actually use to sell your products and services.

After your meeting, they may tell you thanks and to talk soon or to send a proposal. [Send them the proposal and follow up immediately](). Let them know you're thinking about them and you'd like to go over the proposal with them. This is where a lot of people are going to drop off because they don't want to actually spend money. It's your job to make it easy and justifiable for them to give you money since you're helping them with their business.

If they need it, give them space. You're only going to agitate the waters if you are too aggressive. However, you want to have healthy follow up. Give them a week, at most. If they say they need a month to think about it, ask them the right questions like:

- What's holding you back?
- What do you need to start right now?

If they still say they need a month call them in two weeks.

If your follow up is working, you will set up another meeting and expect payment during that time. Ensure all the decision makers are in the room, give one final presentation, and get to work.

Objections

Hopefully, you will encounter people that don't even ask some of these questions and simply accept their ignorance on technology and allow you to do the work. They've probably heard that digital marketing is essential and if you were there at the right time and place you may be the one they have to choose from.

- *"Our customers aren't on these platforms"*
  This is just silly. You're telling me that out of the 2 billion people on Facebook and the 40,000 google searches per second that none of these would be qualified leads for you?

  The truth is, just about everyone and their mother is on Facebook. Everyone especially has at least email and email marketing can be part of your package. Simply tell them the people you have now don't seem like candidates but you will find a new wave of leads once we start this up.
- *"Direct mail is the only platform that works!"*
  I'm sure it works great — but this works better.

  [Calaboration](#) does handle a lot of [traditional marketing](#) like mailers and lawn signs. These methods aren't *bad*, they're just more work, more money, and less effective depending on the industry.
- *"Nobody falls for ads."*
  If no one clicked on advertisements these platforms that rely on ads for revenue wouldn't be in business.
- *"This is way too expensive!"*
  We are a premium agency. I implore you to go with the cheaper agency but we may have moved up in price by the time you want to come back.

  If you proposed your services properly and demonstrated how the client would be making a return on their investment, saying it's too expensive is their attempt at lowballing you or telling you to forget about it and they're not interested. The value you get for digital advertising is too great for anyone to be complaining about pricing and the services you're providing by handling these accounts for them will make them money in their sleep.
- *"It's not the right time"*
  It's never the right time. This is something that builds upon itself and only grows over time. If you're not able to justify the cost and essentially have our services pay for itself, then you're free to drop off.

- *"I have to talk to my partner."*
  I love/hate this one. First of all, why aren't you talking to both of them? The overall decision maker is not there.

  Secondly, you have to convince this one person that the deal is going to be worth it and that their partner would be mad that they didn't just pull the trigger right then and there. Tell them how they'd be doing a favor to their entire company by signing right now and instead of badgering their partner with discussions, they can barrel in with the solution already implemented.
- *"I don't want contracts that I can't back out of."*
  This is actually to benefit you and us. If we were to sign on for a month-by-month deal, we'd be spinning our wheels trying to get you any and every result we can just for the sake of getting you to continue working with us next month. Once we know we have a runway of six months, we can actually do this correctly and figure things out for the long term.

  Don't make the same mistake Jerry Maguire did. You're going to have to put the agreement on paper and lock your client in for a period of time. If they can't understand this, then they have no business running a business themselves.

Business Model Canvas

Your business model canvas (BMC) will be your outline to all the aspects of your business. It'll be the guide that walks you through everything your business might encounter such as where you're sourcing your tech from, who you have to communicate with in order to sell and keep your business afloat, and where your revenue is coming from.

We'll dive into each facet of what the canvas calls for and where everything goes.

Value Proposition

Your value proposition is the value you're providing to your customers. What is the actual service or product they are buying from you and how does it benefit them?

If your marketing agency specializes in Facebook ads for real estate agents, your value proposition is qualified lead generation — these leads should be home buyers or those wishing to sell their home in the near future. If your digital agency focuses on creating video content for political candidates, the value proposition you're offering is high-quality and compelling video advertisements.

The value proposition should be the tagline for what your business is and why anyone should want to do business with you. You're offering something of value and conveying what that is in relation to increasing a client's bottom line is crucial to landing any deals. This is something you must decide on.

Possible value propositions:

- Lead generation
- Digital marketing strategies
- Brand awareness & credibility
- Strategic branding

Customer Segments

Define your ideal client. Who are you selling to?
You might be focusing exclusively on selling to dentist offices. If this is the case, your customer segments are dentists that run their own business. Similarly, if you're targeting small business owners, anyone with a bar, storefront, or other small businesses in your city might be perfect leads to identify in your customer segments.

You may change your mind on many of these things later, but determining one customer segment out of the gate and sticking to a certain plan will help grow your business since there is no ambiguity regarding who you should be spending your time on.

Possible customer segments:

- Real estate professionals
- Small/medium-sized business C-level executives
- Entrepreneurs
- Startups
- Marketing directors

Channels

How are you reaching these customers? The surest way of getting in front of most of your prospects is by networking. *That* is an entire channel that belongs in this section of the BMC because it defines the channels in which you're finding your clients.

Whether you're doing cold outreach, emails, trade shows, or

discovering new and creative ways to reach out to your prospects, there are many channels that can contribute to how well you market yourself and your business.

Calaboration has gathered many great leads from merely posting content on existing forums and demonstrating knowledge in the field. This is an entire channel that is very underutilized since it doesn't scale well.

Possible channels:

- Trade shows
- Business meetups
- Online ads
- Forums

Customer Relationships

What is your relationship to these customers? This can range from no contact to immense contact. You might be meeting with your clients every day or never see them in your life. SaaS products have the luxury of not dealing much with individual customers while agency owners do have to be present much of the time.

How closely are you working with these customers? Are they involved in your creative process or do they allow the agency to handle everything from idea to implementation? Deciding on how you and your agency interacts with its customers is crucial or else you'll be running a company where some clients are favored over others and where no one truly knows where to go next.

Possible customer relationships:

- Trust — customer is disconnected from the process
- Co-creation — customer is involved in the creative process and sees the entire project develop

Revenue Streams

Where you are you getting money and what is it for? This should be one of your top priorities — after all, you have no business if you have no revenue. Determine where your money is actually coming from and what it takes for you to make that money.

If you're selling web design, your revenue is decided by how many websites you're building. If you're selling political consulting, your revenue is decided by how many politicians are paying you to tell them what to do!

Possible revenue streams:

- Website design + hosting
- Social media management
- Consulting

Key Resources

What do you need to run the business? The great thing about digital agencies is that they can be run from almost anywhere. You can easily and happily build a website or manage digital advertising while on the beach — just as you could on a mountain. This means that your physical resources can remain quite low.

The most common resources are going to be your hardware, equipment, and services. If you're paying for some SaaS products to handle your invoicing and email, these are your resources along with your computer and keyboard. Software will likely be your most popular resource since you may need to be paying for everything from creative and sales software to payment software.

Possible key resources:

- Desktop
- Laptop
- Creative software
- SEO tools

Key Activities

*What do you need to **do** to serve your value proposition?* This explains what actual actions you're taking to keep the business running. The answer to this one relies on your value proposition. If you're making videos, you need to go out and film. If you're making websites, you not only need to get on the keyboard and start designing, you also need to find clients that will want a website.

Anything and everything that your body does while running this

business is the activities that are required in your BMC.
Popular key activities:

- Film promos
- Design traditional advertising postcards
- Design banner advertisements
- Attend marketing events

Key Partners

Who do you need in order to accomplish all the duties and goals of the company? You can't go at it alone. You'll find early in your digital agency venture that you're relying on many different third-parties to properly deliver to your client. You may be sourcing developers overseas or frequenting the printing shop down the block for mailers. Whatever and whoever you're involving in your business is a partner and they're an instrumental part to your success.
Popular key partners:

- Printers
- Developers
- Film editors
- Copywriters
- Political consultants
- Real estate consultants

Cost Structure

What are your costs? Whatever you're paying for belongs in this section of the BMC. You probably will be getting an office eventually and have tons of bills to pay — these are all sunk costs that are necessary for the business. Equipment and outsourced work will act as costs as well when you're determining what your actual profits are.
Popular cost structures:

- Web hosting + management
- Printing
- Media

- Development

Week Three: Step by Step

1. **Land a meeting**
   It shouldn't be difficult to convince someone to let you buy them a coffee so you can talk business. Keep it casual but always be selling. You're there to build connections right now — that's it.
2. **Follow up**
   The biggest thing that separates the good salespeople from the poor ones — followup. Stay on top of your prospects and don't let anyone fall through the cracks. You'll be happy you reached out to someone just as much as they are happy that you reached out.
3. **Continue cold calling**
   Remember, doing things that no one else is doing is where your largest opportunity is. There are a lot of people cold calling for web design, but if you truly take advantage of it there's a way to game the system.
4. **Work on your BMC**
   I don't want you to spend too much time on this since it doesn't generate revenue, but it's still very important to go through the exercise and determine all of these facets of the business before you start growing.
5. **Follow up**
   Just keep doing it!
6. **Send your first proposal**
   Congrats! Hopefully, you were able to get this far in the process of meeting and selling to the point where you're finally able to craft all your services and prices on a document and send it over. You're on your way to closing deals and making money.
7. **Close a deal**
   Remember that proposal you sent earlier? You just closed the deal. Whether you're winning or losing deals shouldn't worry you too much yet. You're going to send out some

proposals that never get answered again and you're going to get clients that don't even want to wait for the proposal to begin your services — everyone's different.

Week Four: Operating Your Digital Agency

Now that you're finalizing what your agency is doing, selling people on the idea of what you can provide, and finally getting checks cut for you to do these things, you have to perform and actually give the results you're promising.

What you're actually going to be doing for your clients is less relevant than the results you're promising them — keeping this in mind will be crucial to your success since you can always switch up your strategy and game-plan to provide the results.

Operating your digital agency will include things like strategizing marketing plans, executing on web development and advertising campaigns, and most importantly, understanding the needs of all types of businesses you're working with.

Understand Your Client's Business

Depending on what kind of client you have, you have to understand their business first and foremost. You're not going to be required to take a whole medical exam if you're working with a physical therapist, but you should know enough to be able to be qualified to work as a front desk operator at the office.

Researching the industry is crucial. If you're going to be selling gym memberships through online advertising, you better know the standards that have been put into place throughout the years by other gym memberships services nearby. Doing some due diligence and learning how other businesses are doing this is a great idea and will give you an idea of how you can proceed.

You better know the services that are being offered through the gym. If there's a yoga class every Saturday and Wednesday morning, you should know about that offer and know about the benefits of yoga. If you're unaware of the benefits of yoga, you'll have no idea how to market this nor who to market it to. If you're unaware of when these classes are, you'll have no chance of driving foot-traffic whatsoever.

You are, effectively, the business's marketing director. They can't afford someone in-house so you're what they've decided is best for their budget and trust you to deliver on what you promised.

Know Their Audience

If you're going to start generating business for other companies, you need to understand who they want to do business with.

Who is their ideal lead? If you're working with a mortgage lender, their clients are real estate agents with homebuyers or the homebuyers themselves who want to find their home through the lender.

If you're working with a local bar or pub, their ideal customer is someone who might want to come through for happy hour and dinner.

If your client is a carpet cleaning service, they'll need homeowners who yearn for a clean house.

If your client is a political candidate, they'll need a lot of difficult-to-quantify brand awareness and GOTV efforts — their audience is voters and there's no way to guarantee votes.

Ultimately, the benefit of knowing the audience of the business you're working with is more important than anything else the very business could even provide you with. Hopefully, they'll have a clear and solid understanding of who their customers are — if they don't, that just became your job.

Free work

Sometimes you'll have to suck things up and do some free work when you're very first starting out. I cap you at one free job during your startup. It'll be very easy to get caught up in some people until they take advantage of you and before you know it, you're spending enough time and energy that should be worth thousands or even tens of thousands of dollars on these people for free.

The reason we even suggest doing one free job is that you can maximize the opportunity if you're smart. Some of the free work [Calaboration](#) did when initially starting out were from some high-profile clients who were more than happy to refer us to their high-profile friends after they saw how well we did.

You will get no benefit out of making a personal blog for the college student who is trying to be the next online influencer — they have no connections nor an audience at all to even see your work. Anyone that is telling you to do work for free for them because of the exposure is out of touch with reality and should be avoided. Exposure does not pay bills and unless you have the same sized audience as Hollywood or The White House, your exposure is worthless.

Doing work for free can benefit you and harm you at the same time. As mentioned above, you leave yourself prone to being taken advantage of. Once you perform some free work and the consumer enjoys it, they may expect you to keep going without paying. Anyone with common decency wouldn't do this, of course, but they're out there.

Good connections will greatly appreciate your free efforts and do all they can to get you leads, show off your work, and talk you up to all their friends. If they're not doing this, you failed at some point during the prospecting stage and did free work for someone who was undeserving of it.

It's crucial that your free work is great and that you're not skimping on your performance just because it's pro bono. Ensure that you're also invoicing the clients getting free work with the original cost. There is no reason they shouldn't see on paper how their website costs $5,000 normally but they got an incredible deal — this will keep anyone from feeling you did them a favor and remind them that this is still a business transaction.

Track Work and Results

You want to ensure you're tracking everything you're doing and recording all the results you're bringing in for free clients. This is so you can build a case study out of your work. You want to be able to show off this work and get as much exposure as you can for it — or else, it was all for nothing.

Building your case study will be fun and rewarding. This is when you show off every little thing you did for this client. Every lead that comes through the door, every [page you built on their website](), every photo you took as part of their media package — whatever it is they needed from you. You are explaining in detail how you came in and got these results so everyone reading knows what you and your agency are capable of.

Tracking results and quantifying everything in your business is a good idea whether this is a free or paid client. Case studies should be built for most of your clients so long as they agree to it and the work is exceptional enough to display.

Contracting

To truly capitalize on your business, you'll have to spend more time making sales and building connections than doing the actual work required to keep your clients happy. The good news is that just about anyone can handle SEO and email marketing but only you can go out there and win clients with your broad knowledge and industry expertise.

    Fortunately, since you've established a process and created productized versions of your services, it will be very easy to scale and take on new employees that can go through these motions. At the end of the day, things like web development and SEO can be done by most anyone. Your clients are paying a premium for your understanding of their business mixed with your expertise in the services you're providing. Once you syndicate that out to your team who can handle the management, maintenance, and daily workloads, you are truly running a business that is sustainable, solvent, and scalable.

    The challenges you'll run into when deciding on who to hire will be to vet their skills and ability to communicate. Those that are experts at SEO might be terrible at answering your calls and emails — this is a red flag when deciding to bring them on the team.

Similarly, those that interview well and are incredibly good at getting their point across might fool you into thinking they're more skilled than they actually are — this is a great skill for a salesperson to have and good news for the person interviewing, but sometimes difficult for the person on the other end of the table to decipher. Self-awareness and the ability to pinpoint someone's true value will come in handy in times like these.

Contracting work out at first is the wise thing to do. Once you grow you'll be in a better position to hire anyone full or part-time. In fact, you may not even have the volume of clients to bring anyone on 1099 in the beginning and you may have to resort to using freelancing service providers so you can rid yourself of any messy tax issues. These services are great when it comes to smaller objectives like weekly blog posts, Facebook ad management, and even spinning up websites when you're in a crunch.

The true value of your agency is not the commoditized services it provides, it's the volume and prestige of clients you are able to sign.

To really scale and to enable you to spend your time running the business instead of working in the business you must outsource work and understand that others can do it better than you. Your job is to manage, run a company, and sell — do not get romantic over the idea of staying in the weeds of these accounts' marketing tactics because it will only slow you down when the priority of really growing the company should be your main focus.

Execution

If you're just starting out and want to make some quick cash before building out a team of outsourced developers, you'll have to plan, strategize, and execute on your digital services yourself. This can mean anything from running Facebook ads for a local pub, building a website for your municipality's town hall, or creating mailers for a real estate agent's open house. These are some of the most common services with the highest demand that you should be selling as part of your digital agency.

Web Design

You are not selling websites. You are selling a marketing tool that lives and thrives on a domain in a server. No one will care that you created custom technology that makes your websites lightening fast with moving pieces and flashy banners. They certainly will not care what platform you use and only really want the final result which is a working website that has their contact information and operating hours on it.

Many times, you'll find your clients don't even know what they want on their website. They know they need a website and they know you could build it for them — that's as far as they'll go regarding the design and content of the website and the rest is up to you.

Thankfully, you know their business. You know that the perfect website for a healthcare representative will have a lead generating form, content regarding different plans they have, and contact information in case any visitors have questions before moving forward with their services.

Your agency is getting paid to fix a problem that the client does not even want to think about. It would be foolish for a high-performing real estate agent to learn how to build a website when they could have spent that same afternoon selling a home. Their time and money are much better spent outsourcing that facet of their business to you. Keep this in mind when you're pitching your services because unlike large tech companies, most of your clients will never care about the technical achievements of the website.

The very first website you'll have to build if you haven't already is your agency's site. This is where you can keep a blog, display previous work you've done, and generate leads for future projects. Here's the entire checklist we use at Calaboration that highlights each step and tool to use for all of our websites (this assumes you have a server spun up and ready to be build on):

- Install WordPress
- Login using your credentials
- Visit *Themes* and delete each one except whichever one is active
- Visit *Widgets* and delete each one
- Visit *Pages* and click "add new" just to get a feel for the program
- Visit *Posts*. Posts and pages are very similar but pages are used to be static such as your contact page or about us page. Posts are dated and are fed into the blog portion of the site in reverse-chronological order.
- Visit Admin > Settings > General and ensure your email is entered.
- Visit *Themes* again and install a new one — we at Calaboration stick to Astra Themes and are very happy.
- Visit *Plugins* and click "add new":
    - Astra Sites
    - SMTP by WP Forms
    - iThemes
    - Yoast
    - Elementor
- Choose a site from Astra Starter Sites and any other necessary plugins will be automatically installed
- *Appearance > Customize* will allow you to choose colors and determine branding for your site. Your fonts and logos should complement these well.

- Visit a page and click *Edit with Elementor* to enter the page builder where you can easily drag and drop elements and build your site in a WYSIWYG environment.
- Configure your emails settings using SMTP
- Create contact forms
- Generate a sitemap using Yoast
- Share your site

We recommend using WordPress for your websites. Hosting providers are a dime a dozen; so do some searching and find one you're happy with — these should literally cost you $50 per year to keep the site up and running. Keep in mind, you are likely charging your clients *at least* $99/mo to host their site. This is pure profit for your agency since the cost of hosting a site is extremely low and your personal maintenance is only a couple hours per year to ensure the site isn't crashing down.

Calaboration currently has over 20 websites on our hosting packages. This means the business is making $4,000 per month on nearly completely passive income alone. Just like real estate, hosting and management fees are some of the best subscriptions going. They know the second they stop paying they lose their website — just like the second you stop paying your rent you lose your roof.

Between selling the website at a premium and charging for hosting, this can be an entire business on its own. A premium price for a website could be anywhere from $5,000 to $50,000 and much higher. I've sold websites for as little as $1,000 when I was building Calaboration but very quickly realized what people were actually willing to pay. Thankfully, we have more skills that we can up and cross-sell to these prospects as well.

Digital Marketing

[You are not selling digital marketing](). You are selling brand awareness, lead generation, tickets to an event, or whatever the objective might be. Similarly to your website, no one will care what kind of Facebook and Google ads you're running. They won't have any desire to see the copy or creative content you decided to go with. They only want to see the results of your efforts that increase their bottom line.

Digital marketing is a very broad and difficult-to-define term since it's more of a genre. Technically, managing someone's blog could be considered digital marketing since SEO falls under that. I've never packaged SEO or web design in with digital marketing and it takes some educating of the client for them to realize what is what. By the end of the chapter, we go over the package and pricing plan Calaboration offers for reference.

If digital marketing could be anything from designing a website to strategizing a marketing campaign, for the purposes of this we'll define digital marketing as running paid advertising.

Strategizing a Paid Traffic Campaign

Crafting ads, designing creative and compelling content, and targeting audiences that will click and buy from these advertisements are some of the most important facets to any business. This is in your hands when you pick up a new client and pleasing them with results and quality work should be a big priority in your agency.

Facebook advertising gives us a great template to work off of regarding the areas of focus for your marketing. It includes everything from the overall campaign down to the granular targeting.

1. **The campaign** is the big picture. There can be one or hundreds of separate ads running under one campaign. You probably notice campaigns when you see a new wave of ads coming from a big company that all follow a similar theme.

    "Look at all these elderly couples enjoying our diner food — you can be one too!"

    This diner might have a dozen ads featuring a new couple in each one. This is different from their campaign last year that focused on high school sports teams celebrating victories at the diner. These are all campaigns that focus on the main idea and execute different types of storytelling.

2. Many people argue **targeting** is the most difficult part of online advertising because it can most easily make or break your entire campaign. If you're showing ads for running sneakers to people over 50, you might have a harder time

converting sales than if you were targeting them to 20-year-olds.

If your product or service is so specialized that you need to hit a specific demographic, it's your job to determine who should be seeing these ads and where they are. It's very easy to unwillingly show thousands of dollars worth of ads to people who have absolutely no business buying this or even looking at it.

Conversely, if you're running a billboard in Times Square, you don't care about any type of targeting — your targeting is simply: *anyone and everyone who is walking the streets who happen to look up.* This is the opposite of targeting because they're going for volume. Big brands want every person to see their logo and their latest endorsements because they are for everyone. Everyone might need sportswear, but not everyone needs specialized yoga equipment.

Targeting should be very strategic as well. When marketing and [building brand awareness](#) for a public figure or politician, targeting will be extremely useful because you can modify the narrative based on who you're talking to. If you have a Republican state senator running against an incumbent, it's a great idea to find the Republicans and hit them with ads that outline their conservative beliefs. Further, it's extremely useful to hit the Democrats with ads that outline how you've endorsed Democratic candidates in the past.

Your product (the politician) isn't changing, but the perception is radically different because separate demographics are viewing it around modified narratives — keep in mind, no one is lying, it's literally just marketing.

You'll find many more opportunities to cleverly target your marketing strategies as you learn more about other businesses you're working with and your own. Although people might

say there are too many ads we're hitting a breaking point, the proper targeting is the perfect combat to that.
3. **Creative content** is whatever it is the user is looking at. This could be a post on social media, a video, a shirt on a specific sportsperson, or a billboard on the side of a building. Whatever you are creating for your ad, the visuals and feelings it exudes are what will drive conversions.

Since there are so many types of content you can use in your marketing, you'll have to research and determine what is best for your industry and what has proven to be most successful. Coming in with this mindset will likely help you since you'll then have the understanding of what is normally done and then allowing you to put your agency's twist on it so the campaign is successful.

Real estate agents and politicians love mailers — if you're working with someone running for office or someone with an open house coming up, it'd probably be a great idea to design some postcards to mail out. Physical designs like this are very costly because of shipping and could be a great way to bring in more revenue for the agency since all costs are going through your services.

Video is extremely popular and works very well. Ads with video are going to get many more clicks and give off a more professional feel when users come across your brand. Video production is expensive and, if done wrong, could come out looking extremely amateurish. Taking video anywhere should be considered an investment where you put the time into editing and money into the equipment.

Finally, we have the basic designs that we see on banners, sidebar ads, pre-roll ads, and everything else on the web. These could be photos or illustrated stories. Quality is always extremely noticeable so whatever is executed here must be done properly.

Aside from actual creative is the copywriting content. Quality copywriting is one of the greatest skills on the planet and immensely out of the scope of this book. We do recommend everyone becoming somewhat skilled in copywriting and your ads will thank you. A solid headline could make many more people click your ads and read your website compared to things that are slapped together.

The list can go on a bit longer regarding what can be done inside a digital marketing campaign. We've done things that mix out-of-home (OOH) advertising and digital marketing so that we hit people on all levels. We've even targeted certain people with certain ads consistently through mailers and digital so we can seem like a larger operation than we were.

Gathering all the data and deciding in what order ads should go out and through which mediums is important during your planning phase. Once you decide where things are going to go and where they're going, writing the content and creating the artwork is next. After that, you have a full marketing strategy ready to be executed.

Pricing & Packages

Deciding on pricing is always an exciting area of the business because this is where the revenue comes in. Depending on how large you are, how well connected you are, what bills need to be paid, and many more parameters, your pricing might start at something that you're not happy with — this is fine.

[Calaboration](...)'s first [pricing structure](...) looked something like this:
Web design — $3,000 + $99/mo for hosting
Digital marketing — $950/mo
Social Media Management — $950/mo
SEO — $650/mo
Videography — $750+

These prices gave some people sticker shock and others thought it was too cheap they barely trusted the service. The problem with pricing is that it's completely up to the buyer to decide how they feel about it. On top of that, it's arbitrary enough that you can decide whatever you want to charge. These prices above have changed many times and have gotten much higher because the people we're doing business with are expecting to spend tens of thousands of dollars on a website over only a few thousand.

This goes back to perceived value. The website we create for

$3,000 is not much different than the one we created for $10,000 — the only difference was the industry in which these websites were used in and the clients' ability and willingness to pay more money.

If you're a single person who is trying to get money for next month's rent, you may have to make some serious modifications to whatever pricing plan you hope to use. There is nothing wrong with selling a website for $1,000 to someone who is not willing to pay any more than that. That one deal will fund you the rest of the way until you make more impressive deals in the near future.

Only turn down work when it's not worth your time and there's no ROI. The only website Calaboration would build for $1,000 right now is if it's a donation or helping a family member. It's merely not worth our time to work on anything with that kind of budget.

The next thing to consider when building out your pricing plan is the clientele you're expecting to attract with it. People who have smaller budgets are more difficult to work with — this has been proven time and time again and anyone you speak to who is working in the services industry will likely agree immediately.

Designers have this problem a lot because they are constantly micromanaged from their clients. It's not worth your time to sit and be directed by the client unless they're paying even more than if you just did the entire project by yourself. Those clients that are only spending a couple thousand dollars on your website will be the ones that are typically micromanaging and expect every single bang for their buck possible. The ones that are dropping tens of thousands expect your agency to do everything — this is the way it should be.

Week Four: Step by Step:

1. **Land some free work**
   Like we stated, you want to try and get the best possible bro bono job you can. This will allow you to worry-free take care of a job, make some friends, and give you a project you can start marketing the results of.
2. **Strategize your marketing timeline**
   Figuring out what goes where and when it goes there will be a time-consuming project within your agency at all times.

This is the work you're getting paid so handsomely for — do it well.
3. **Perform the work**
Once you're done strategizing, you'll have to hop on the computer and start the actual marketing. This won't be too bad and should be a day's worth of work for most clients — until you have to change things and re-strategize.
4. **Build a case study**
All that work you did now gets showcased. You documented the process of what you did for this client and you're ready to put it on paper so you can show the world how talented you are.
5. **Continue outreach**
It's very important that you're not getting too consumed with the work and all the different facets of the business. You should partition your time accordingly such that you have enough time for outreach as well. Once you finish the first project, you're going to need more work to do — you're only going to have more work to do if you have a full pipeline.
6. **Show everyone, and their mother, this case study**
You not only worked really hard on the client's needs, but you also worked really hard on the case study itself. Show it off and use it as your primary marketing piece to pick up more clients.
7. **Build a million dollar agency**
It takes time, but it's absolutely possible. You can do it.

Final Words From Nick

Well done! I'm hoping you followed along with the vision of replicating these steps for your own agency. These tactics will work but not overnight. It'll require some hard work on your end but the rewards will show themselves eventually and once they do you'll wonder how you ever worked a 9-5 before. It's truly a mind-altering situation when you find how easily you can make real money by doing what you love and helping other businesses grow.

With everything we talked about, this should be a great opener to start working on your own agency.

It's cheap, efficient, and yields great rewards if you do it correctly — so long as you're keeping your clients pleased and performing at impactful levels, you will grow in your niche and become a household name in the industry. Ensure you're not rushing and allow for the market to gravitate toward your business — people will become inbound leads if you are following the system correctly.

Always Be Closing!

Once more! The process relies very heavily on your ability to close business and win clients. This is easy if you're just being yourself, demonstrating authenticity, and acting in a professional manner.

Go in meetings and events like the authority you are, educate people around you, and become a good person to know — once you consistently do this you will be an unstoppable and invaluable force in the industry.

Thank You!

I hope you enjoyed this guide as much as I enjoyed writing it. The art of building agencies and growing businesses is something I'm incredibly fond of and I hope to do it more effectively each and every day.

Be sure to visit f EntrepreneurialEfficiency.com, our Facebook Page, and even join the group where you can find other agency founders in the process of starting up, picking up their first clients, and even far along enough they're hiring and finding office space.

If you haven't already, feel free to follow on Twitter as well. Thanks again, good luck, and I can't wait to hear more about your success!

Disclaimer & Copyright

Finding Oneself by Nick Calabro
www.entrepreneurialefficiency.com
© 2018 Nick Calabro
All rights reserved. No portion of this book may be reproduced in any form without permission from the publisher, except as permitted by U.S. copyright law. For permissions contact:
nick@entrepreneurialefficiency.com
Ebook ISBN:

www.ingramcontent.com/pod-product-compliance
Lightning Source LLC
Chambersburg PA
CBHW040320220526

45473CB00009B/2506